THE ECCENTRIC
GARDENER

First published in Great Britain in 2005
by PAST TIMES®, Oxford, England

Typeset by David Onyett, Publishing & Production Services,
Cheltenham

Cover and design by Peter Wilkinson
Printed in China by Imago

PAST TIMES

Contents

Introduction

It has been said that 'if you scratch an English man or woman underneath you will find a gardener'. One could add, 'scratch the gardener and you will find an eccentric'. What is more, the rule would seem to be true worldwide and not confined just to our shores.

The word 'eccentric' has a sliding-scale built into it. At one end it is a euphemism for just plain potty, at the other it describes a person or behaviour that is off-centre, or out of skew with convention.

In *The Eccentric Gardener* you will meet characters from both ends of the scale and several who sit comfortably between the two – those who are just delightfully dotty.

It would be unfair to refer to Bishop George Law as barmy, even if he did believe that in his garden was proof positive of the story of the biblical flood and Noah's Ark. Similarly, James Mellor's allegorical garden in Cheshire was born out of a deep religious faith and a longing to share his beliefs with the wider world (although, unlike Bishop Law, he did so freely).

It is tempting to categorise the surrealist devotee, Edward James, who created a fabulous garden in Mexico, as mad – but one should take heed of someone who knew him well. Salvador Dali dismissed the idea, on the basis that James was too calculating to be insane.

One also has to consider that behaviour that would be perfectly acceptable in the modern age was considered completely eccentric in days of old, and so men like Sir Joseph Paxton are included.

One of the great maxims in the gardening world is that 'money makes the best manure' and certainly there have been any number of fabulously wealthy men and women who have poured their purses into their gardens. The American press magnate, William Hearst, spent millions on his estate in California and, in the century before, William Beckford at Fonthill in Wiltshire spared no expense whatsoever.

Then there are those who are not so much mad, as just mad about plants and nature in general. Dame Miriam Rothschild may have had odd sartorial tastes but her views on natural gardens and wildflower meadows have been adopted worldwide. Reginald Farrer, also, had some peculiar mannerisms and habits but he is now recognised as the 'Father of Rock Gardening'.

Conversely, aristocrats such as Sir George Sitwell and George Durant appear harmless and amusing, and yet there was another side to their personalities that proved not to be so funny to their families. Durant, from Tong Castle, for example, was hated by several of his children and took his ideas a little too far when he insisted that the only way for his seven-year-old son to learn to swim was by being thrown, fully-clothed, into the lake. The boy drowned.

What links all these characters is their desire to express their personalities through their gardens (or in the case of the botanical artist, Margaret Mee, through her paintings) and the following pages are a celebration of their whims and fancies.

One suspects, however, that they represent many more anonymous souls who reading on will recognise that they too, could be well be classified as eccentric gardeners.

Flights of Fancy

Dyed Doves & The Mad Boy

Anyone familiar with Nancy Mitford's novel *The Pursuit of Love* will know that her character, Lord Merlin, was based on Gerald Tyrwhitt Wilson, the 14th Baron Berners who was even more eccentric than his fictional counterpart.

Diplomat, composer, artist and writer, the highly talented Lord Berners was also a born prankster and the tales of the jokes he played on family, friends, foes and unsuspecting members of the public are legendary. This was the man who had a clavicord fitted into his Rolls Royce, whose Dalmatians wore diamond collars and who enjoyed meals 'in which all the food was of one colour pedigree, i.e. if Lord Berners' mood was pink, lunch might consist of beet soup, lobster, tomatoes, strawberries'.

At his home, Faringdon House in Oxfordshire, Lord Berners' eccentric tastes were indulged to the utmost. On the front door a framed notice advised 'It is requested that all hats be removed', an elaborate chandelier hung *outside* the house, one of the bedrooms boasted a glass four-poster, and having read that in China doves were dyed with food colouring, Lord Berners decided to do the same. Consequently the Faringdon flock fluttered in all the colours of the rainbow.

In 1935 the generous baron commissioned the last major folly to be built in England. The site was already known as Folly Hill and so Lord Berners decided to put up a tower which would give some meaning to the name. 'The great

point of this tower,' he said 'is that it will be entirely useless.'
The architect, however, had not fully understood the brief
and Lord Berners was dismayed to discover on his return
from holiday that his tower was more modest and classical
than he had hoped for. He insisted on adding mock
battlements and various gothic flourishes and for good
measure had a sign added that read: 'Members of the public
committing suicide from this tower do so at their own risk'.
The 140-foot-high folly was a twenty-first birthday present
to Lord Berners' love, the bisexual Robert Heber-Percy,
known as 'The Mad Boy'. (Far from being pleased 'The
Mad Boy' was disappointed with the tower. What he had
really wanted was a horse!)

While the folly on Folly Hill and the interior of Faringdon
House reflected the tastes and quirks of its master, the
garden was the domain of the equally eccentric Heber-
Percy. There were the manicured lawns one would expect
of a stately home but the row of stately urns that bordered
the gravel sweep at the front of the house were filled with
plastic greenery rather than the real thing; a statue of one of
Britain's military legends, General Havelock, was half
submerged in the lily pond because Heber-Percy thought
there was nowhere else to put it; the changing room floor
of the crenellated swimming pool was inlaid with thousands
of pennies and the pool itself was guarded by two
enormous stone wyverns.

When Lord Berners died in 1950 he left all of his estate to
Heber-Percy who bequeathed it when he died thirty-seven
years later to his only granddaughter.

Pyramids and Progeny

In 1954 what was left of Tong Castle in Shropshire was demolished to make way for a new motorway, but the extraordinary tastes and passions of one of the castle's former owners lives on in local legend.

George Durant II inherited his father's estate, and the fortune he made in Havana, in 1797 when he was just twenty-one. The Moorish-Gothic mansion appealed to the young man's taste, but the gardens, designed with the help of the famous Capability Brown, certainly did not match the new squire's personality.

George was rather taken with pyramids and so he had two erected, each ten feet high, on ten-foot-high gateposts either side of the main drive. Not content with that, he had an ornamental pigsty built in the shape of a pyramid, and several years later treated his chickens to a similar edifice – although this one was inscribed with various entreaties such as 'Scratch Before You Eat'.

The famous willow tree fountain at Chatsworth might well have been the inspiration for Durant to have a similar 'tree' installed at Tong Castle. Made of iron, with water pipes secreted in the trunk and branches, any unsuspecting visitor who took rest on the seat beneath the 'tree' could be immediately drenched.

In the fashion of the day George built a hermitage and while the first inhabitant lasted seven years in the employ of the Durants, the second did not make it past four weeks. By their very nature, hermits were required to live in solitary confinement but George, by all accounts, adopted a worldlier attitude. He built a pulpit by the gatehouse so that he could preach to passers-by, and to ward off anyone tempted to poach on the estate he put up a large archway made of whales' jawbones. He also had iron harps hung in various trees around the estate so that when the wind blew the harps would wail disturbingly – supposedly as a further deterrent to trespassers.

Durant's energies, however, were not limited to dreaming up weird and wonderful contraptions for his estate. His first wife gave him fourteen children, his second six and he reputedly sired a further thirty-two in the local village – virtually one in every household – all of whom he sponsored as god-children. When the first Mrs Durant finally left the family home in high dudgeon over her husband's affairs he contested her demands for financial support. He eventually managed to reduce the settlement to two hundred pounds a year and, to celebrate his success, erected 'a hideous monument within sight of the castle – a monument which two of his sons blew up with seventy pounds of explosives on the night he died'.

In 1844 yet another George Durant took over the castle but his tenure was short and the entire estate was sold off eleven years later to the Earl of Bradford.

Acrylic Arcady

It all began with a single daffodil but then Clifford Davis's garden in Lancashire grew to be a riot of colour all year round. There was no weeding required, no need to cut the grass and no danger of plants dying, as nearly everything in the pensioner's garden was made of plastic – and what was not plastic was concrete or wood.

The green corrugated plastic 'lawns' were studded with countless daisies, marguerites, roses, anemones and numerous imaginative flowers that Clifford created over the years using any bits of plastic he could get his hands on. He was nothing short of inventive. Painted cotton reels became daffodil trumpets, sauce bottle tops were beaten out to become petals, and in Clifford's hands there was no telling what a detergent bottle could become. In fact, anything that could be adapted was – as long as it was made of plastic.

A plastic shower tray became a duck pond, complete with cheerful plastic ducks, and while most gardener's greenhouses are a mass of seeds and fledgling plants, Mr Davis's overflowed with various plastic objects – many with bits cut out of them.

Originally the Davises' garden in St Annes, near Blackpool, was very much like any other small suburban garden. Mr Davis put the transformation down to a plastic daffodil he found in a neighbour's dustbin one day. He retrieved it, took it home, spruced it up and planted it among the patch of real daffodils yet to bloom. The dazzling effect was captivating and Clifford's imagination was set in motion.

According to Jane Owen, in her fascinating book, *Eccentric Gardens*, Mr Davis 'lived an odd sort of life'. He was, at various times, a farmer, a milkman, a café owner, and a miner. He even once attempted to become an inventor but his 'flying bicycle' never really got off the ground.

The reactions to Clifford Davis's garden were always mixed, as you can imagine, but Mr Davis loved the fact that it was all his own creation – so much more reliable and exciting than a traditional garden and 'youngsters love it'.

Recycling in Beverley Hills

In an expensive Los Angeles suburb you can find yourself transported to Asia by simply walking into the garden of an extraordinary house called Dawnridge. It was the home, and is now fast becoming a shrine, to the celebrated American jewellery designer, Tony Duquette, who with his artist wife created, among other things, an elaborate Indonesian village in their backyard.

Duquette, who spent years as a film and stage set designer, worked on the principle that if 'some is good, more is better'. He and his wife Elizabeth, nicknamed Beegle, travelled extensively and collected voraciously. They sent back from their journeys through Europe, Africa and Asia any item that caught their eye to add to the extravaganza that is Dawnridge. Once home, items such as the elaborately horned Nigerian Ekoi headdress would be displayed unexpectedly – in the case of the headdress against an eighteenth-century painted Italian screen.

Yet Duquette was a master of invention – look among the pagodas, bridges and stilted houses that fill the Eucalyptus dell at the rear of Dawnridge and you will find 'a frieze made of skateboards, towers made of oilcans and pagodas made of light fixtures'. Some items – such as giant obelisks – are from stage and film sets yet many are entirely of Duquette's creation. He was a master at recycling. To the unimaginative, Air Force temporary air landing strip sections might not have great potential, yet in Duquette's hands they became filigree panels and look for all the world as if they have been transported from a master craftsman's Asian workshop. He said that he did not like to reproduce what already exists. 'I'd rather take a shell, a rock, a tree branch and a grill, and use them to create an angel or a chandelier.'

The planting at Dawnridge is also exotic, and most of the lush shrubs and plants are grown in pots to allow for versatility – irrespective of the fact that they all need to be hand watered.

When Duquette died in 1999, his business partner, Hutton Wilkinson, who had started work with Duquette when he was still a teenager, inherited the property. More than 8,000 objets d'art and items of furniture were sold off and now Dawnridge is to become a showcase for items made only by Tony Duquette and Beegle. One gets the feeling that Mr Duquette would approve.

The World and a Coffin

There is any number of Victorian reformers who took it upon themselves to improve the lot of the common man and the Reverend John Alington was no exception. Owner of Letchworth Hall and estate in Hertfordshire, a farmer and keen gardener, Alington was determined that his workers should enjoy the fruits of his knowledge.

Having made several alterations to the traditional manor house (including what is referred to as 'a large but unmeaning tower') the Reverend had a pool on the estate converted into a scale model of the world. All the continents were represented and the good man would have his workers row him around and around while he lectured them on geography. Such trips were then supplemented by further lectures, quizzes and discussions.

Alington gained a reputation for being a most generous host and welcomed all manner of people, from all walks of life and levels of society, into his home. If his visitors were on horseback, no matter – as the Reverend did not insist that they dismount before entering his drawing room where he enjoyed singing lustily while accompanying himself on his grand piano.

Another of his favourite entertainments apparently was to be carried aloft around the Letchworth Hall garden in an open coffin – to what end is unclear.

In line with his principles of education, Alington once decided that the estate workers would benefit from a trip to the Great Exhibition in London in 1851. His only concern was that the confusion of the capital would prove to be too much for them. Consequently he had the men fashion a model of London streets 'covering the area between Hyde Park and Kings Cross', so that they could be prepared for the adventure. He devised that half of the group would learn the way to the Exhibition from the station and the other half the return journey. The former group were to wear a ribbon on their right legs, the latter on their left. It would appear that the exercise did not come up to the Reverend's satisfaction, however, as the excursion was cancelled.

At the time that John Alington ruled Letchworth Hall the nearby village had few facilities and a population of under a hundred. One suspects it would please him to know that less than forty years after his death his little corner of Hertfordshire was developed as the world's first Garden City in accordance with the vision of Ebenezer Howard, a prominent social reformer. And in keeping with Alington's hospitable nature, Letchworth Hall is now an hotel.

National Pride

Some people are not consistently eccentric but have flashes of inspiration when their less conventional side comes to the fore. If such people happen to be gardeners, the effect can be quite surprising.

Take Sir Francis Henry Goldsmid, for example. Part of a notable finance dynasty, he was the son of the first Jew to be made a Baronet and in 1858 became the first Jew to be called to the bar. He later went on to become the MP for Reading, founded the Jews' Free School, did umpteen good works and was generally a pillar of society. In 1864 he bought the Rendcomb estate in Gloucestershire, demolished the house and built a fine mansion. His quirkiness only really showed when it came to landscaping the park. This he had laid out in the form of all twenty-two letters of the Hebrew alphabet from aleph to tzaddi – a design that could only be appreciated in full from the air.

Decades later neighbouring landowners in Somerset also used their estates to confirm their allegiances to anyone who happened to be flying past. One gentleman, Auberon Hubert from Pixton, had a wood laid out in the pattern of the Union Jack in response to his neighbour, Otto Gardiner, who had had his woodland felled in parts to create a giant swastika. Gardiner was apparently a member of the Cliveden Set – some of whose members were strongly suspected of harbouring pro-German sympathies in the run-up to World War II. (The name comes from the Cliveden Estate near Maidenhead, home to the Astor family which was embroiled in the controversy.) It is claimed that Mr Gardiner was under the delusion that should the Luftwaffe undertake an intensive bombing campaign over Somerset his home would be spared.

It was pure patriotism however, that inspired a family in Bermuda to build a relief map of the island territory in their garden. The prominent Gibbons family has all the islands with the parishes defined amid the lily pond and, while the garden is private, the pond is open to the public. (As a matter of interest, the miniature Bermuda is reached through a 'Moon Gate' – a traditional piece of architecture in the islands. These large round arches are said to bring good luck and happiness to any newly married pair who pass beneath. You can find them all over Bermuda – the idea being imported from China in the mid-nineteenth century by a local sea captain who had seen just such a thing on his travels.)

One of the most important and beautiful gardens in Ireland also displays its creator's patriotic zeal. When Edith, Lady Londonderry moved to Mount Stewart in County Down on her marriage, she thought her husband's home to be 'the darkest, dampest, saddest place I ever stayed in'. With boundless enthusiasm and energy she set about rectifying the matter. Her talents show to their full effects in the garden where she created different compartments varying from the traditional to the exotic. The eighty-acre garden mixes up all sorts of architectural styles and planting which is said to be 'compelling'. There is a lily wood, the Temple of the Winds, a Peace Garden and one section of the garden is laid out in the shape of a shamrock. There is a harp – the symbol of Ireland – in yew topiary and along the top of a yew boundary hedge a family hunting party is in full chase.

The Londonderrys' ancestry is also commemorated. It is believed that one of their antecedents was the first O'Neill who raced against an opposing clan from Scotland to make it to Ulster. The finish was close and in a desperate bid to lay claim to the prized land, O'Neill cut off his right hand and threw it onto the shore. This extraordinary act is commemorated in Lady Londonderry's garden as a huge hand planted out in dark red begonias among the gravel.

Devotion and Dentures

The small Northumberland village of Branxton is not the first place you would think of if you wanted to see a giraffe, pandas, hippos and Winston Churchill in close proximity. However, in the surprising Fountain House garden you can see all these and much more besides.

Known as 'The Concrete Menagerie' the garden behind the unassuming semi-detached village home was created by an old man to delight his disabled son. John Fairnington married late in life and his only child, Edwin, was born with cerebral palsy. The Fairningtons rejected the idea of sending their boy to an institution and cared for him at home. When John retired in 1961 at the age of eighty the family went on holiday to Scotland and, when Edwin was rather taken with some animal statues that they saw, his father decided that he would make some for their own garden. (Fairnington had been a master joiner and was more than useful with his hands.)

At first he started making small statues and then he called on the services of a friend and former colleague, James Beveridge, to help. Together they filled the garden at

Fountain House with an eclectic mix of concrete statues, including the fourteen-foot-high giraffe. Picture books provided all the inspiration the men needed and John Fairnington drew up life-sized plans.

There is a wonderful variety of exotic animals alongside sheep, horses, cattle, stags, rabbits and replicas of some of Fairnington's heroes. Winston Churchill complete with a cigar is only a few yards away from Lawrence of Arabia sitting proudly atop a camel. (The camel's wide smile is courtesy of a set of Edwin's mum's false teeth.) A local sheepdog champion kneels beside his dog and there is a shrine to Robbie Burns with suitable quotations marked out in gold Letraset. Paths wend their way around the statues while low-growing evergreen shrubs complete the picture.

Edwin was apparently delighted by his garden and in nine years John Fairnington created nearly 300 statues and fitted them all into just under an acre of land. When Edwin died in 1971, John Fairnington built a Memory Corner for his son and then laid down his tools.

Now Fountain House is the property of John Fairnington's nephew and namesake and the family open it to the public for all to enjoy.

Gnomania

We have the Germans and Sir Charles Isham to thank for garden gnomes. The Germans, because they first made them, and Sir Charles because he was the first person to bring them to England in the mid-nineteenth century. Sir Charles, from Lamport Hall in Northamptonshire, had inherited his Irish mother's love of gardening and when he inherited the estate he set about adding to what she had already created.

He installed an Italian garden and an extraordinary rock garden that rose up twenty-four feet from the surrounding parkland. As well as a plethora of plants which included such exotica as pygmy fir trees, there were extra touches to the Lamport Hall rockery such as a toy monkey swinging from one of the dwarf conifers and twenty-one china gnomes.

Sir Charles had bought the gnomes when on a trip to Germany and it is said that for him they were not just amusing garden ornaments but held some sort of religious significance. A dedicated spiritualist, he held a firm belief in the supernatural and faithfully recorded his various sightings of 'fairies' and 'ghostly miners'. To Sir Charles his gnomes were supernatural beings.

When Sir Charles died, his daughters, who did not share their late father's enthusiasm for the little men, had them all removed – except for one which had fallen, forgotten, into a crevice. 'Lampy' as the mislaid gnome is now known, was found years later and given place of honour in Lamport Hall as well as the status of being insured for a million pounds.

The eccentric and fun-loving Sir Frank Crisp of Friar Park in Henley was another ardent gnomophile. He had a special cave built for his collection, and while Isham's gnomes were nearly all in classic poses such as digging, Crisp's little fellas got up to all sorts of things. The Crisp gnomes took snuff, sat atop champagne bottles pulling at the corks and huddled together to examine a fly. Some of them have, in more recent times, also rubbed shoulders with the rich and famous. The former Beatle, George Harrison, took on Friar Park in the 1970s and featured some of the Crisp gnomes on the cover of his solo album *All Things Must Pass*.

Ann Atkin's gnomes lead a far more sober life. The former hippie art student – now a grandmother – owns and runs the Gnome Reserve in Devon that she set up in 1979. It is home to more than a thousand little people, many of them made to her specifications. At West Putford you can find gnomes in church, gnomes having a tea party and gnomes enjoying the seaside, in fact gnomes leading very full, if not particularly exciting, lives. Mrs Atkin's passion for gnomes apparently started in the early 1970s when gnomes began to pop up in her dreams and they still figure in her paintings which include 'gnomes in their cosmic universe'.

Much of the Gnome Reserve is old beechwood with a convenient stream running through and the rest is the Wild Flower Garden bursting with about two hundred and fifty species of wild flowers, herbs, grasses and ferns – nearly all labelled. Fairies, attached to stakes, frolic among the plants. Mrs Atkin's philosophy is written up for all to appreciate:

'Our natural British heritage we try to preserve.
All generations like to come and observe'.

In coming to observe visitors are encouraged to wear red caps provided for just such occasions 'so as not to embarrass the gnomes'.

Knole and Tin Delphiniums

The turbulent and unconventional life of the poet, author and gardener, Vita Sackville-West, has long intrigued, but her mother was an equally eccentric soul.

Victoria Josepha Dolores Catalina Sackville-West was born the illegitimate child of Lionel Sackville-West, a British diplomat, and an Italian dancer, Josefa Duran – also known as 'Pepita'. In spite of the fact that her parents never married, the young Victoria and her siblings were brought up in a style in keeping with her father's standing and when he was posted to Washington Victoria went with him as his official hostess. She took the local society by storm and later claimed to have received twenty-five offers of marriage during her time in America.

As the youngest son of the family, Lionel Sackville-West had not expected to inherit but when his older brother died he succeeded him to the family baronetcy and Knole House, the splendid Tudor mansion near Sevenoaks in Kent that had been the Sackville-West home since 1603.

It was at Knole that the young Victoria met and fell in love with her first cousin, also rather inconveniently called Lionel, and despite much opposition she married him in 1890. The younger Lionel joined his new bride and his uncle at Knole and life continued much as before. The younger Sackville-West's daughter, Victoria Mary Sackville-West, known as Vita, was born two years later, the only issue of the marriage. (Victoria was not impressed and thought her daughter ugly.)

When Victoria's father died her husband succeeded to the baronetcy and life at Knole went on unchanged, dominated by Lady Sackville's extraordinary whims. She was a woman who could be either wantonly extravagant or extremely miserly, depending on her mood. Not in favour of buying writing paper she utilised whatever was at hand and apparently had a particular penchant for the lavatory paper from the ladies' room at Harrods.

She was also obsessively fond of fresh air and during her reign refused to allow fires to be lit at Knole – irrespective of the temperature. Meals were 'al fresco' and dinner guests 'were obliged to wrap themselves in fur coats and place a hot-water bottle on their laps'.

A beautiful, spirited and difficult woman, she resisted her husband's attempts to divorce her and eventually relinquished her hold on Knole only when she was forced to do so upon her husband's death. When Lady Sackville-West did leave the house to go to her new home in Brighton, however, seven vanloads of furniture went with her as well as statues by Epstein, a sculpture of her by Rodin (who thought she was wonderful) and a diamond necklace made up of forty-two stones.

Anxious to maintain standards Lady Sackville-West resorted to dreaming up schemes to boost her own coffers. One of her 'charities', of which she was reputedly the only benefactor, was supposedly to help 'The Homeless Sleeping on Brighton Beach'. She had greater success when she decided to run a white-elephant stall (again for her own benefit) and thought it would be an attraction to have a real one. Lady Sackville-West wrote to the only person she could think of who might have such a thing – the King of Siam. The good gentleman obliged by sending her not a real white elephant but a small one made of solid silver.

As she aged, Lady Sackville-West's eccentricities became more marked. At Knole there had been gardeners; in Brighton there was no such luxury. Instead Lady Sackville-West developed a taste for tin delphiniums which she pronounced to be 'impervious to slugs'. However, in unusual deference to her daughter, whenever Vita was coming to visit, there would be a flurry of activity and the otherwise bare beds would be filled with artificial flowers. The gesture did little to improve the turbulent relationship between mother and daughter and Lady Sackville-West died a lonely death at White Lodge in Brighton in 1936. Ten years later the fourth Lord Sackville passed on her beloved Knole to the National Trust.

Stately Splendour

Glass and Gumption

Chatsworth, the ancestral home of the Dukes of Devonshire, is one of the most magnificent estates in England yet the splendour of its garden still owes much to a man who was born into poverty and started his working life as a farmhand.

There are those who consider Joseph Paxton to be 'one of the most remarkable self-made men of the Victorian era' and even those who would not go so far cannot deny the extraordinary influence of the man with boundless energy and vision.

Paxton's association with Chatsworth came about because the Devonshires' London estate included the Chiswick Gardens Arboretum, leased by the Horticultural Society, where Paxton had found himself work as an under-gardener. Paxton often would open the gate for William Cavendish (the sixth Duke) as he passed through and they came to discuss garden design and horticulture in general. Devonshire was apparently very impressed by the young man and when Paxton was only twenty-three he was appointed Head Gardener at Chatsworth. It was to be a long, happy and highly productive appointment and the two men became lifelong friends.

William Cavendish, the 'bachelor' Duke had not shown any particular interest in gardening until he met Paxton, but once he had been introduced to the delights of horticulture he was hooked.

Together they set about transforming Chatsworth. The
work did not always receive public approval and many of
the developments were considered distinctly odd. John
Claudius Loudon, an eminent landscape designer of the day
and founder of *Gardener's Magazine* was particularly
scathing. He considered Paxton's new flower gardens at
Chatsworth to be in far too 'highly enriched architectural
taste', thought the notion of growing flowers in the kitchen
garden quite eccentric – 'we would as soon introduce a plot
of cabbages in the newly-formed parterre at the house' –
and deplored the use of gravel for the walks.

Undeterred the Chatsworth pair continued on, confident in
what they were creating. Fuelled by Paxton's love of plants
the Duke sent out expeditions to the East and the Americas
to bring him home new and exotic varieties. To house
them Paxton built the Great Conservatory – the prototype
for his larger and grander Crystal Palace that was to come
ten years later.

People travelled from around the world to marvel at the
enormous and avant-garde greenhouse at Chatsworth and
the Duke loved it. According to the current Duchess of
Devonshire, 'It covered just over three-quarters of an acre.
The surface area of the roof was 52,277 square feet and the
24,560 sash bars measured about 40 miles.'

The Great Conservatory is no more – it was pulled down
in 1920 on the orders of the ninth Duke having fallen prey
to the lack of men to tend it and coal to heat it during
World War I. Paxton's grandson supervised the sad job. Yet

much of what Paxton did create has survived. It was he who decided to relocate the hamlet of Edensor as he thought it ruined the view from the house and the 'new' hamlet of Edensor bore, and still does, several idiosyncratic Paxton features. You can find a Swiss style chalet, Tudor chimneys, Italian windows and the entrance lodge resembles a small fort.

He planted an arboretum as well as an eight-acre pinetum, supervised the largest collection of orchids in England, ensured the dwarf bananas were properly cared for and devised novel water features. The most spectacular is the Emperor Fountain – built in honour of Czar Nicholas, the Emperor of Russia and friend of the Duke. The fountain is a marvel of engineering and, using gravity alone, can send a jet of water 296 feet into the air. Unfortunately the Czar cancelled his trip and never saw the fountain but it remains named after him to this day.

Paxton eventually took on the supervision of all the Devonshire Estates, became involved with railways, newspapers and Parliament and still found time to design the revolutionary Crystal Palace – the Millennium Dome of its day – to house the 1851 Great Exhibition. The structure that began as a doodle on a piece of blotting paper was six times the size of St Paul's Cathedral and took 2,000 men six months to build. It also secured a knighthood for Joseph Paxton.

It is worth noting that before he died in 1843 John Claudius Loudon had changed his mind about Paxton and praised him in no uncertain terms for his services to botany and gardening.

Brown but not Brown

Viscount Petersham, later to become the fourth Earl of Harrington, was a man with particular tastes. Something of a dandy, Charles Stanhope enjoyed clothes and it was suspected that, to look his best, he wore corsets to show them off to advantage. Distrustful of tailors, he preferred to cut out his own clothes to ensure the perfect fit and even designed a jacket – known as a Petersham – that the then Prince of Wales copied, having one made for each day of the week. (The style of hat that Stanhope invented did not, however, gain royal approval and enjoyed but brief popularity.)

One of Stanhope's other little peculiarities was that he was obsessively fond of the colour brown. Everything from his horses and carriages to his servants' aprons and boots had to be brown.

Maintaining strict sartorial standards and a spot of soldiering kept the Viscount busy until he was fifty, when within a very short space of time he inherited Elvaston Castle in Derbyshire, succeeded to the Earldom and took on a wife. The new Countess of Harrington, formerly an actress, was considerably younger than her husband, and he decided to redesign the gardens for her as a lavish wedding present. It was a project that was to last more than thirty-five years and involve more than eighty gardeners.

Capability Brown (such an appropriate surname under the circumstances) unfortunately declined to take on the project and it was down to the ever patient William Barron, formerly of the Edinburgh Botanical Gardens, to meet the Earl's demands. These included planting and maintaining more than eleven miles of evergreen hedges, supervising the building of a curious temple that has been described as being 'Sino-Moorish-quasi-Gothic', creating an Alhambra garden, a French garden, grottos, rock gardens and countless conceits. It is not recorded what the Countess thought of her wedding gift but others have called it 'an outrageous phantasmagoria'.

When the Earl died at a grand old age, his widow returned to London and the house passed on through the family. Nowadays the Elvaston estate is owned by the Derbyshire County Council and the gardens have become a public country park.

The Matterhorn and Rock Music

Of all the lavish gardens of the early twentieth century there is one that stood – literally – head and shoulders above the rest. Built by the larger than life Sir Frank Crisp – a leading lawyer, botanist, horticulturalist, microscopist and landscape gardener – Friar Park at Henley boasted its own scale-model of the Matterhorn as the centrepiece of its large rock garden.

Sir Frank began work on the garden before he set to on his mansion – a 120-room Gothic extravagance of turrets, gargoyles and towers – and the rock garden was his passion. He brought in 7,000 tons of stone from Yorkshire and set his men to the job. The thirty-foot high mountain had to be reshaped several times before it met with Crisp's approval and was finally topped with a piece of rock from the Matterhorn itself. Just like the real thing there were also waterfalls and more than four thousand alpine plants to complete the scene.

Once the rock garden was in place, Sir Frank turned his attention to creating a number of other exciting features for his garden. There was an Ice Cave with blue icicles and a statue of a Chinese stork, a Skeleton Cave complete with skeleton, and a Vine Cave hung with enormous bunches of grapes that contained electric lights.

And then there were the friars. Crisp had something of an obsession with friars and they popped up all over the garden and the house: there was a friar in the Illusion Cave, friar gargoyles on the outside of the house, friar light switches (which involved twisting the noses of the carved figures to turn on the lights) and sculpted friar lamps.

The main lake at Friar Park was also designed to amuse. It was built in three staggered layers but only the top part of the lake was visible from the house and the terrace. Across the middle layer Sir George built a bridge which, because it was below the level of the top part of the lake, could not be seen from the house. This created a remarkable illusion when viewed from the house: anyone crossing the bridge seemed to be walking on water. To give the same impression, Sir Frank had stepping stones placed just under the surface of the top part of the lake so that the butler could be summoned from the lower reaches of the garden and appear to 'walk across' the lake to serve drinks to his startled guests.

After Sir Frank Crisp's death the gardens at Friar Park fell into a state of disrepair until an unlikely saviour came along in 1971. The estate was bought by the former Beatle, George Harrison, who threw himself into restoring Crisp's fun-filled paradise. Along the way the famous rock star also wrote and recorded *The Ballad of Sir Frankie Crisp* in dedication to his predecessor at Friar Park.

Egotism and Italian Style

The name Sitwell and eccentricity could be considered synonymous, especially in relation to Sir George Sitwell – father of the talented literary trio, Edith, Osbert and Sacheverell. While Dame (as she was to become) Edith Sitwell claimed, 'I am not eccentric. It's just that I am more alive than most people. I am an unpopular electric eel set in a pond of goldfish', there was no doubt her father had full claim on the adjective and has been called 'an example of English eccentricity at its finest'.

Sir George, who inherited his baronetcy when he was only two years old, had a typical English upper-class education (Eton, Oxford) and at the age of just twenty-five was elected to Parliament. However, while he was undoubtedly a clever and astute man, he is remembered more for his egocentric and erratic behaviour.

He was passionate about medieval history, genealogy and landscape gardening and it was at the family seat, Renishaw Hall near Eckington in Derbyshire, that his horticultural fantasies were first played out. He was a great admirer of the classical Italianate style and vehemently opposed to anything that smacked of the Romantic. His plans for Renishaw were elaborate and, at one stage, it is claimed he employed 4,000 men to dig out an artificial lake in the grounds. (Sir George supervised their progress from precarious wooden towers that he had erected around the garden to afford him a bird's-eye view of the work in hand.)

Sitwell was forever dreaming up grand schemes and his eldest son, Osbert, once wrote of his father, 'He abolished small hills, created lakes, and particularly liked to alter the levels at which full grown trees were standing. Two old yew trees in front of the dining-room window at Renishaw, were regularly heightened and lowered; a process which I believe could have been shown to chart, like a thermometer, the temperature of his mood.'

One of Sir George's more absurd ideas was to stencil willow pattern designs on the rumps of his herd of white cattle so as to improve their rather dull appearance. Unfortunately the experiment was short lived as the beasts refused to stay still long enough for the artist to complete the work.

Nonetheless he retained his enthusiasm for farming and once even proposed to pay Sacheverell's fees at Eton in pigs and potatoes. (The offer was declined.)

Sir George was a great believer in his own talents and, so that the world might better appreciate the correct way to do things, in 1909 he published, *On the Making of Gardens*, a book that has been described as 'an argument for imaginative thought in garden planning'. (While Sir George wrote various other books, including the *History of the Fork*, and *The Errors of Modern Parents*, his gardening tome was the only one to make it into print.)

He was a man who was constantly dreaming up new schemes and remained undeterred when some of his more bizarre ideas failed to impress. His musical toothbrush and his miniature revolver for shooting wasps may not have found general favour, but they afforded him great amusement. He would often sit out on the terrace at Renishaw taking pot shots at unsuspecting wasps 'with limited success but enormous satisfaction'.

Of his talented progeny, Sitwell was dismissive. Although Edith, his eldest child, was (and still is) highly acclaimed as a poet, he said he thought she would have been better to go in for lawn tennis, although when she was young his advice was slightly different. 'There is nothing,' he said, 'that a young man likes so much as a girl who's good at the parallel bars.'

As for gardening it remained a passion all his life and it was one of the few pursuits in his life that bore fruit. His gardens at Renishaw – still the home of the Sitwell family – bear his stamp to this day, as do the gardens at Castello di Montegufoni (Castle on the Hill of the Black Hawk), a property in the heart of Tuscany that Sir George bought in the early twentieth century to further his interest in the Italian style.

Montegufoni comprised two palaces, five villas, armouries, chapel and bell tower, as well as thirty-six acres of garden, olive groves and vineyard. The possibilities for Sir George were very appealing as was the fact that there is reference to the castle in Dante's *Divine Comedy*.

While Sir George's relationship with his family never ran smoothly and he considered it 'such a mistake to have friends' there was one man, his valet, Henry Moat, who was devoted to him. Moat, whom Osbert described as 'an enormous purple man like a benevolent hippopotamus' was wont to say that 'Sir George is the strangest old bugger you ever met' – history would seem to agree with him.

Citizen Kane and the Enchanted Hill

Roughly halfway between San Francisco and Los Angeles is one of the most extravagant interpretations of an Italianate garden in all of the United States – if not the world.

La Cuesta Encantada (The Enchanted Hill), more commonly known as Hearst Castle, was the creation of the fabulously wealthy press tycoon, William Randolph Hearst.

It took nearly thirty years to build the mansion and gardens, said to have been inspired by the tour he made as a young boy with his mother around the splendours of Europe.

Everything at Hearst Castle is on a grand scale – the estate itself spreads across 270,000 acres and the drive alone is nearly five miles long. At the height of the Hearst era 700,000 annuals were planted every year and more than 2,000 varieties of trees and shrubs were grown in the nurseries on the estate.

One of the most written about controversial and influential men of his day, Hearst has been portrayed as an evil opportunist, a fascist, an egocentric of gargantuan proportions and, more kindly, as an 'eccentric individualist'. Certainly the man, who, one employee said, had 'a voice like the fragrance of violets made audible', was no shrinking violet and stories abound of how Hearst imposed his will. He was a zealous gardener with definite ideas and permission had to be granted before his gardeners could do as much as cut a branch from an overhanging tree.

The fanaticism that he applied to the construction of Hearst Castle typified the life of the man who it is said was the inspiration for the film *Citizen Kane*, a story about a megalomaniac 'ill at ease with himself despite his riches'. There are countless stories of how Hearst, or 'The Chief' as he was called, flouted convention. As the instigator in America of what, in England, would be called 'tabloid journalism', Hearst was not one to let facts get in the way of a good headline. It is said that when one of his photographers was sent to Cuba to capture the conflict he reported back that he couldn't find any war, to which Hearst replied, 'You provide the pictures, I'll provide the war.' Another one of his employees recalled how Hearst reacted when presented with the latest copy of one of his papers, '... he spread the proofs on the floor, and began a sort of tap dance around and between them ... The cadence of it speeded up with his reactions of disturbance and slowed down to a strolling rhythm when he approved. Between dances, he scribbled illegible corrections on the margins and finally gave the proofs back to me.'

With the development of Hearst Castle he demonstrated a little more patience and lavished time and money on the project. At one point the bills were mounting up so rapidly that he was forced to sell property elsewhere to cover the costs.

Hearst's ally in the project was his architect, Julia Morgan, one of the first women architects in the States and a devotee of the Italian style. Together Hearst and Morgan created a landscape designed to interest all year round. Italian cypresses are a constant theme. There are Canary Island date palms and giant California oaks and overwhelming displays of 'rhododendrons, oleanders, camellias, azaleas, eucalyptus, agapanthus, glossy green citrus trees with fruits sparkling in the sun and brilliant purple lantanas'. In keeping with Hearst's grand designs there are also countless statues and hard landscaping features, the most notable of which is the extravagantly classical

Neptune Pool, used as a part of the set for the film *Spartacus*.

Due to ill health Hearst left La Cuesta Encantada in 1947 and the project was never entirely finished, yet it remains a towering symbol to what dreams and money can achieve.

William Randolph Hearst died in 1951 at the age of eighty-eight and six years later Hearst Castle was given to the State of California to become one of the region's most visited attractions.

Folly de Grandeur

The legendary eccentricities and excesses of William Beckford, who inherited so a vast a fortune that he became the richest private citizen in Britain, stand as a lesson, to any who need it, that money does not buy happiness.

Born into a wealthy family in 1759 William was indulged in a manner his mother considered appropriate. Only the best would do for William and so, for example, Beckford had Mozart for a music teacher (the musical prodigy was, himself, only a child at the time) and was introduced to such luminaries as the French philosopher Voltaire.

Surrounded by all the splendour of the family home the young squire of Fonthill grew up with every advantage but little rein on his petulance or 'unbridled temper'.

Then, when he was nineteen, William's mother sent him on a tour of the great English estates to encourage a taste for country pursuits. It was a disaster. The tour not only strengthened his intense loathing of blood sports but he met and fell passionately in love with William Courtenay, the eleven-year-old future Earl of Devon.

Beckford made no attempt to hide his feelings and the relationship developed over the years – even when William took the pretty Lady Margaret Gordon for his bride. (It is said William adored his wife and was devastated when she died in childbirth only three years after their marriage.) It was around the time of Margaret's death that the affair with young Courtenay finally became public and to escape scandal and retribution William fled to Europe.

For the next thirteen years William Beckford was an itinerant, although he was seldom alone. His entourage consisted of 'his doctor, his maitre d'hotel, baker, cook, valet, three footmen and twenty-four musicians'. (As you would expect, he also travelled with his own bed, crockery and cutlery.) His reputation did little to endear him to fellow English travellers but he was well accepted by the European nobility who must have been bemused by his extravagant whims. On one occasion, for example, Beckford thought the view from his window from a villa in Portugal was sadly lacking so 'to improve the view' he imported a flock of English sheep.

When eventually Beckford did return to England he threw himself into the business of embellishing Fonthill in a lavish manner. Still blacklisted by society, Beckford chose to surround the estate with more than fifteen miles of twelve-foot-high walling and began the business of building the most remarkable folly of a home that England has ever seen.

Beckford's inspiration came from Salisbury Cathedral, yet Fonthill Abbey, as it was officially called, is perhaps the most famous building disaster of all time. James Wyatt was employed as the architect and hundreds of men were taken on to undertake the job. Beckford insisted they should work on a shift system so that building could continue twenty-four hours a day and as encouragement he plied the men with drink. The combination of exhausted and inebriated workmen, shoddy craftsmanship, shabby materials, an unsuitable design and Beckford's impatience did little to ensure that the structure would be long-lasting. The three hundred-foot octagonal tower at the heart of Fonthill fell down three times before it finally stayed put long enough for Beckford to believe it was secure.

At the same time William set about creating the right surroundings for his 'Castle of Atlas', as he called the Abbey and the garden that he lavished his fortune on is considered to be one of the finest examples of the time of 'natural' landscaping. Artificial lakes were dug, more than a million trees were planted and there were lavish displays of shrubs and flowers. There was a 'Norwegian hut', a rosarium and a 'thornery' as well as glades, avenues, caves, grottos and dells. The effect was dazzling.

The creation of the lakes Beckford took extremely seriously. He employed his former art teacher, the celebrated artist Alexander Cozens, and took him to Italy so that he could sketch Beckford's dream – Lake Nemi, the crater of an extinct volcano in the Alban hills. In Italy, the superb towers of the Castelgondolofo rose above the waters of the lake, and Beckford wanted to create the same impression back at Fonthill. Cozens painted several views of the lake and, in due course, the scene was recreated as closely as was possible with Bitham Lake on the Fonthill estate. The one exception to this otherwise carefully copied view was that because of his extensive planting it was only Beckford's tower that was visible from the lakeside rather than the whole immense building.

When the Abbey was more or less complete in 1813, Beckford said of it, 'the Abbey cannot be contemplated without emotions that have never been excited by any building erected by any private individual in our times'. What Beckford might not have expected was for those emotions to be ones of frustration and anger. Certainly the Abbey was large enough to house the enormous collection of art, furniture and objects d'art that Beckford had built up over the years, but that was, arguably, its only advantage. The chimneys smoked, the wind whistled through the windows, the roof leaked and the state of the tower foundations threatened its imminent collapse.

Nonetheless Beckford continued to live in seclusion in his Abbey in the company of 'a Spanish dwarf, his heraldic advisor and his four dogs', as well as a retinue of servants.

Several years later when Beckford's financial affairs took a decided turn for the worse, he sold Fonthill for £300,030 and moved to Bath. The Abbey's new owner John Farquhar, a munitions manufacturer, also had eccentric leanings as well as money and ignored all Beckford's warnings about the construction of the building. When, three years later, the octagonal tower finally did collapse, Farquhar said only that it made Fonthill a more manageable size.

Eventually what remained of Fonthill was demolished but William Beckford's garden has never been equalled. According to Christopher Thacker in *The History of Gardens*, 'What he had undertaken was beyond the scope of ordinary rich men and, more importantly, beyond the scope of the garden itself.'

Nature's Own

Queen of the Fleas

The highly esteemed and charming Dame Miriam Rothschild gained her soubriquet through her dedicated and lifelong fascination with this otherwise vexing parasite. She sat on various high-powered academic committees, published more than 300 scientific papers and wrote numerous books on a variety of subjects, but her great love was the flea. She was a robust and dedicated researcher and often kept live flea samples in cellophane bags in her bedroom to stop them 'being annoyed by children'.

She was born in 1908, the eldest daughter of Charles Rothschild, the younger son of the first Lord Rothschild. Charles Rothschild thought that formal education stifled natural intellectual creativity and so he oversaw Miriam's early education at home, firing her fascination with fleas, butterflies and nature in general. Although her father died when she was just fifteen years old, Miriam inherited his passions and her overwhelming interest and enthusiasm for nature in all its guises knew no bounds.

Miriam did not marry until she was thirty-five and before the marriage was dissolved fourteen years later she had produced six children. In spite of the demands of family life she continued her work – often late at night when the children were in bed.

Miriam belonged to a family that has produced many passionate gardeners over the past two hundred years who have had the money, knowledge and flair to create magnificent parks and gardens throughout Europe. While elsewhere Rothschild trademarks are manicured parklands, extravagant flower beds and elaborate topiary, Dame Miriam's garden was the complete opposite.

She was a vehement opponent of cruelty to animals and her home and garden at Ashton Wold in Northamptonshire reflected her passions and talents in equal measure. She veered away from conventional gardening and said that 'guests, on driving into the courtyard, look at the tangle of unkempt plants and wonder uneasily if they have come to the right address'.

Dame Miriam adored roses and one of her favourites was the dog rose – which she considered to be 'a blissfully untidy plant'. Wild-flower meadows replaced formal lawns, wild roses mingled happily with cultivated varieties, and poppies, cornflowers, and corn cockles thrived in her borders. The entire garden was home to a veritable menagerie, while her greenhouses provided homes for rabbits, butterflies, hedgehogs and orphaned foxes. It is said that Dame Miriam's consideration of her animal charges was limitless and often caught her guests unawares. Once, apparently, when Princess Alice, Duchess of Gloucester came for lunch at Ashton Wold she was surprised to discover a fox sitting comfortably on the chair beside her.

Dame Miriam was delighted when her uncle, Walter Rothschild, a noted natural historian and zoologist, bequeathed to her several giant Galapagos tortoises, 500 parakeets and a Pyrenean hound.

Her eccentric tastes were also reflected in her personal style. She chose not to bother with what she dismissed as 'unnecessary choices' and the frills of femininity. Her preference was to wear tennis shoes in summer, moon boots in winter and white Wellington boots for the evening. Leather was not an option. (She was a vegetarian and a teetotaller – although she never inflicted these personal preferences upon her guests.)

Dame Miriam was also an ardent campaigner for nature conservation and even produced her own wild-flower seed mix, which she named 'Farmer's Nightmare' to promote the cause. She took exception to how the countryside had evolved and sought to counteract the bland, flowerless fields that she compared to 'living on a snooker table'. Thanks to her efforts wild-flower meadows were introduced into more than a thousand school grounds in 1995 and her ideas were taken up at all levels of society. (Prince Charles incorporated her ideas when planning his garden at Highgrove.) In turn, Dame Miriam saw her own garden as living testament to her ideals, 'The Ashton Wold garden has come to symbolise the new sympathy with wildlife. The battle with weeds, the conquest of Nature is a thing of the past.'

During her ninety-six years, Dame Miriam Rothschild received numerous awards including the Victoria Medal of Honour – the highest accolade of the Royal Horticultural Society.

Zoophilist Extraordinaire

One of the most heralded eccentrics of the nineteenth century was a certain Charles Waterton, known as Squire Waterton of Walton Hall. A gentle, fun-loving man, he was noted at an early age for displaying a genuine love for and understanding of all animal and birdlife – with the sole exception of the brown rat, a species he hated with an intense and irrational loathing.

The squire's passion for nature gained full expression when he inherited the family estate in West Yorkshire: rather than enhance the formal gardens and parkland, Waterton proceeded to encircle all 300 acres with a high wall to create England's first animal and bird sanctuary. The move was considered distinctly odd by his neighbours, as was Waterton's habit of inviting his guests to scale the highest trees to inspect hawks' nests and suchlike.

All animals (except, of course, brown rats) and birds were welcomed by Waterton who had a particular fondness for hedgehogs, once kept a three-toed sloth in his room and, at various stages in his life, lavished attention on a Bahia toad and a deformed duck that had been hatched on his estate.

Waterton always prided himself on his ability to endure physical hardship and after his young wife died in childbirth early on in their marriage he took to the unheated attic. He dismissed a bed as 'an absolutely useless luxury' and chose to sleep on the floor. He had a wooden pillow for his head, an old cloak for bedclothes and the windows were permanently open to allow bats and owls free entry.

When he was not off travelling – his other great passion – Squire Waterton would be up before dawn to climb his trees and study the birdlife of which he kept extremely thorough and detailed accounts throughout his long life.

Climbing of any form never worried Charles Waterton, who remained amazingly supple throughout his life. (There is a report that aged seventy-seven he was still able to scratch the back of his head with the big toe of his right foot.)

He was renowned for his almost child-like sense of fun and was particularly fond of hiding under the hall table and pouncing on arriving guests and biting their calves in the manner of a savage dog. His remarkable agility added to the hilarity.

He also displayed unusual taste in taxidermy. When his animals died Waterton enjoyed creating 'new' animals with bits of the various species, which he then put on display around Walton Hall; all the better to unnerve his guests and friends.

In stark contrast, Charles Waterton, a devout Roman Catholic, also gained something of a reputation for saintliness. The writer William Makepeace Thackery contributed to the rumour when he wrote in a magazine article, 'I could not but feel a kindness and admiration for the good man. I know that his works are made to square with his faith, that he dines on a crust, lives as chastely as a hermit, and gives his all to the poor.'

According to Dame Edith Sitwell, in her book, *English Eccentrics*, sainthood was in the Waterton blood, as not only could the family trace its ancestry back to Sir Thomas More, but Charles could also count Saint Matilda, Saint Margaret, Saint Humbert, Saint Louis, Saint Vladimir and Saint Anne among his ancestors.

The esteemed Squire of Walton Hall lived to be eighty-three and while his contemporaries thought of him as a harmless and goodly eccentric, Charles Waterton is now also considered to be one of the first great nature conservationists.

Naturally Yours

William Robinson stands out as one of the great figures in British garden history and was a pioneer of 'natural' gardens, in direct contrast to what he considered to be the Victorian 'pastry-cake' style of the day.

He was born in Ireland and little is known of his early years but by the time he was twenty-one he had worked his way up to the position of foreman of a large country estate – a position he left in rather a hurry. Within the greenhouses under his care were numerous small and tender plants that had been grown from seed and heat was essential to ensure they grew strong enough to be planted out. The story goes that after a blazing row one night with his superior, Robinson took his revenge. He allowed the fires to die out, flung the windows wide open and then set off for Dublin and on to London. It would seem that the incident stayed with him for a long time, for when Robinson eventually made his fortune, and had his own splendid garden at Gravetye Manor in Sussex, he banned the erection of any greenhouse on the property and could never abide a coal fire.

Rather surprisingly, considering the circumstances of his departure from Ireland, the young William found a job at the Royal Botanic Society's gardens in Regent's Park and rapidly rose through the ranks. One of his areas of responsibility at the Society was taking care of the English wild-flower collection and he travelled throughout the country to find suitable specimens. According to Miles Hadfield's *History of British Gardening*, Robinson 'came to know English wildflowers and the English countryside with its cottage gardens, intimately. Indeed it would be no exaggeration to say that he came to love them passionately'. It was through this love and passion that William Robinson conceived his idea of a 'natural garden' where plants could flourish with 'little care or cost'.

Robinson was determined to further his ambitions and within a short space of time he had become an agent for the prestigious nursery Veitch, and learned enough French to be appointed the horticultural correspondent for *The Times* at the Paris Exhibition of 1867.

While William Robinson was without doubt a knowledgeable and keen gardener there are those who contend that his greatest talents lay in writing – and he certainly never missed any opportunities to get his ideas into print. In 1872 he started a weekly magazine called

simply, *The Garden*, and seven years later introduced
Gardening Illustrated, which was much more successful and
ran for forty years.

Robinson also found time to write more comprehensively
about his theories and in all published eighteen books on a
variety of gardening subjects. Most were widely read and
appreciated – *The English Flower Garden* ran to sixteen
editions. His name and ideas became so well known that
the term 'Robinsonian' is still used today to describe
gardens unfettered by formality or convention.

The man himself forged strong friendships and professional
associations in the gardening world and included the now
legendary Gertrude Jekyll among his circle. He helped her
with her garden and she provided plants for his; by 1884
Robinson had amassed enough of a fortune to buy Gravetye
Manor in East Grinstead. His vision was to turn the
immediate garden and its surrounding 200 acres into a living
example of his ideals. There are those who think he did not
quite practise what he preached: among other radical
changes, he moved tons of earth to create a new 'natural'
entrance and felled numerous trees. He did however, over the
time he owned Gravetye, plant 120,000 trees to replace them
and in 1897 alone planted 100,000 daffodils.

For all his views on the natural state Robinson had some
very firm ideas. He demanded that his rhododendrons had to
be banked and that no garden feature should obstruct the
view of the house from the distance. As for what could or
could not climb against the walls of the manor he was again

prescriptive. Only white or pale coloured roses and flowers were allowed.

Such a workload demanded that he employ sufficient gardeners to help him in his task but Robinson was not known for being an easy man to work for. Watching him approach as he strode through his garden, it has been said that his staff never knew from one day to the next if they would be given the sack or a pay rise.

In common with many gardeners, William Robinson had a rather obsessive personality and was a heavy drinker and smoker. Apparently, one day he decided to change his habits and made a point of throwing his pipes into the fire and ordering that he never be served wine again. Always the generous host, however, he insisted that his house guests at the time were offered both wine and cigarettes. However, those who did not come out in sympathy with their host and accept his abstinence 'were served a note on their breakfast trays the following morning telling them the time of the next train to London'.

In spite of his oddities and irascible behaviour, William Robinson carried on his work at Gravetye until he died at the grand old age of ninety-seven in 1935.

A quick-tempered Irish lad who grew to be a world authority on his subject, William Robinson is credited with starting a revolution in gardening and many of the gardens that came after him owe much to his ideals.

Potty About Plants

Daffodils and Miss Willmott's Ghost

Any gardener worth his salt will know the name of Ellen Willmott, even if they know little about her, as so many different plants are named after the woman whom the legendary Gertrude Jekyll described at the time as 'the greatest of living women gardeners'.

Born into a wealthy family, Ellen Willmott first got involved in what was to become her lifelong obsession when she was just seventeen and helped her mother design and plant a formal garden for the family home, Warley Place, in Essex.

Horticulture soon dominated Ellen's life and she used her wealth to sponsor plant-hunting excursions and develop and extend the gardens at Warley Place. She wrote the definitive book of the day on roses and spread her influence by helping redesign her sister's gardens at Spetchley Park. When the Shakespeare Birthplace Trust took on Anne Hathaway's cottage it was Ellen Willmott who was called in to design the garden, and even today *Potentilla* 'Miss Willmott' can be found among the lush and lavish Victorian borders.

Ellen delighted in growing newly imported plants for the first time and it was estimated that just before the outbreak of World War I more than a 100,000 varieties and species grew at Warley – but even that was not enough.

The indomitable Miss Willmott also designed and developed an extensive garden at Boccanegra, on the Italian

Riviera, so that at one stage she had employed a hundred gardeners both in England and abroad. Patient men they must have been because at the same time as gaining renown for her knowledge of plants Ellen Willmott also gained a reputation for being imperious and bossy. It is claimed that any of her gardeners who allowed even a single weed to appear among her precious plants faced instant dismissal.

As well as keeping tight rein on her staff she was also rather fond of spreading her favours in a rather unusual manner. Ellen always carried a pocket full of eryngium or sea holly seeds and delighted in scattering them in her friends' herbaceous borders whether they wanted the plant in their garden or not. In remembrance of this extremely annoying habit the plant is still commonly known as 'Miss Willmott's Ghost', for she remained 'Miss Willmott' all her life.

Her devotion to horticulture cost her not only a marriage but also her fortune, yet it has been said that 'her descent into bankruptcy never interfered with her purchase of any rare plant she coveted'.

As Ellen's fortune plummeted her strange habits increased and she took to carrying a revolver in her handbag and arranged a variety of booby traps around Warley Place. One of her more spectacular arrangements was a series of wires around her daffodil display that if tripped would set off a number of air guns strategically placed to blast the intruder.

Ellen Willmott died in 1934 and her home, and the garden she had so assiduously created, were sold to pay off her debts. Today Warley Place is a nature reserve and Ellen Willmott's name lives on in the innumerable plants named in her honour, and in the cultivars named after her precious garden.

Husbands and Horticulture

The title of Ganna Walska's memoirs, *Always Room at the Top*, gives some indication of the aspirations of the beautiful Hanna Puacz who was born in 1887 (give or take) in Brest-Litovsk, Poland. Determined to become an acclaimed opera singer, the young Hanna started by changing her name to Ganna (the Russian version of Hanna) Walska (Polish for *waltz*, her favourite music).

As Madame Ganna Walska she toured Europe and America to much acclaim and landed the first of her six husbands, whom she claimed was the second richest man in Russia. He, like the following five, was divorced along the way but in the process Madame Walska amassed her fortune.

With the encouragement of her sixth and last husband, Theos Bernard (her second American tycoon) she bought, in 1941, the Cuesta Linda estate in Santa Barbara, California. Originally she called the 37-acre estate 'Tibetland', with a view to using the property as a monastic retreat – but there proved to be a scarcity of suitable or willing monks. Undeterred, the feisty Ganna divorced Theos, renamed her estate 'Lotusland' (after the Indian lotus that grew in one of the ponds) and never looked back.

'Lotusland' is considered to be one of the most exotic of
Californian gardens and is home to the world's second most
important collection of cycads – prehistoric plants common
during the Jurassic period when dinosaurs ruled the earth.
(Woody, seed producing plants, cycads are often confused
with palms or ferns although they are linked to neither.)

In creating her paradise Madam Walska called on some of
the most eminent landscape designers of the day but always
insisted that she was the 'head gardener'. Her passion was
for unusual plants grouped in single species: consequently
Lotusland is divided into distinct areas. Cacti, ferns,
dracaena and bromeliads (the pineapple family) abound.
The Aloe garden has at its heart a pool edged with
abalone shells and for the Blue Garden a local bottling
plant scrap-heap provided the blue glass that edges
the paths.

Her voracious appetite for exotic plants, the bigger the
better, was expensive. If there was a plant she wanted she
did everything in her power to get it at any cost. In the
1970s she even sold off nearly a million dollars' worth of
her amazing jewellery collection to finance her last
creation, the Cycad Garden.

Ganna Walska called herself 'an enemy of the average' and
everything she did reinforced her hatred of mediocrity.
Even when she was in her nineties and unable to walk
without the aid of sticks she would tour the entire estate
twice a day to ensure things were as she wanted.

When she died in 1984 she left her garden and her fortune to the Ganna Walska Lotusland Foundation and the Los Angeles Museum of Art was bequeathed her entire wardrobe.

Ganna Walska's niece, in Gordon Taylor and Guy Cooper's book, *Gardens of Obsession*, is reported to have said, 'My aunt was famous for many things. Famous for her jewellery. Famous for her costumes. Famous for her great beauty. Famous for her husbands. And now famous for her garden.'

Moonflowers and Watercolours

Photographs of Margaret Mee, the renowned botanical artist, show her to have been a very feminine, delicate woman with a twinkle in her eye — but as she herself said, she had a great deal of 'resistance'. It is perhaps just as well, as in all she braved fifteen expeditions deep into the Amazon forest to record and collect the flora and fauna of the jungle.

Margaret and her husband, Greville, also an artist, moved to Brazil in the early 1960s having fallen in love with South America several years before. Surrounded by exotic and unusual flowers, Mrs Mee began to paint them. She also began to venture into the coastal jungle to capture rare species in her sketch book before they were wiped out by the extensive deforestation programmes. Then, when she was in her late forties, she made her first real expedition deep into the Amazon interior.

It was to be the first of many. Leaving her husband behind
in São Paulo, frequently for months at a time, Mrs Mee
would pack a pistol, brushes, paints and sketch book and set
off in a small boat, often with only a local Indian guide for
company.

Her fear was not of the insects, spiders, snakes, animals or
the local Indian tribes, with whom she got on very well,
but of white adventurers or 'semi-civilized humans' as she
once referred to them. There was a notable occasion when
Mrs Mee pulled her revolver on a drunken gold-digger
who made the mistake of entering her hut. The Indians
were most impressed at her bravery and thereafter, she said,
'I was treated like a queen'.

She lamented the loss of the forest and was terrified that
the wholesale destruction of the trees around the Rio
Negro would be copied elsewhere. To her their loss was a
tragedy. 'I almost knew the trees as friends, individually. Not
one of them is left.'

An intrepid and determined woman, Margaret Mee was the
first woman to scale the south side of Brazil's highest
mountain and stopped at nothing in her search for rare and
as yet undiscovered plants.

For more than twenty years she harboured a special dream
– to capture with her paints an elusive cactus that only
flowers one night in the year and then fades. In what was to
be her last trip up the Amazon, in 1987, she succeeded.
Margaret Mee's drawings of the *Selenicereus Wittii*, or the

Amazon Moonflower, are among the forty sketch books, 400 folios of illustrations and fifteen diaries that she accumulated over the years. She was highly regarded as both an artist and botanical recorder and produced several books and staged several important exhibitions. She once said that she needed six lifetimes to satisfy her passion but the one she had was cut short when she was killed in a car accident on one of her trips back to England. A trust was established in her memory and still dedicates itself, as she did, to promoting education and research in Amazonian plant life and conservation.

Rocks and Hard Places

In a remote corner of Burma, above the village of Kawnglanghpu near to the Chinese border, lies the grave of a determined and singular Yorkshireman. Reginald Farrer was only forty when he died in 1920, 'his strength and spirits sapped by the incessant monsoon rains', but in his short life he had done much to enliven British gardens.

His passion was for rock plants and it began when, as a boy, he would scramble over the fells near to his home at Ingleborough Hall and spend hours roaming the family estate. Both Reginald's parents were keen gardeners and encouraged his interest, perhaps thinking it would compensate for his lack of companions. (Reginald was born with a cleft palate and harelip and to save him from the rigours of public school, he was educated at home.) In spite of several operations in his youth he had difficulty communicating and until he was well into his teens his mother was the only person who could understand what he said.

Nonetheless, in keeping with family tradition, Reginald went up to Oxford and, his studies apart, helped to create a rock garden at St John's College. He also wrote incessantly to his mother back at Ingleborough detailing all she had to do to maintain his precious rock gardens and what new specimens she had to find.

When he graduated from Oxford Reginald returned to Yorkshire and established his own nursery. He then set off on his travels to find rare and unusual plants to propagate within it. He lived for a while in Japan and travelled extensively throughout the Orient looking for new plants, the seeds of which he would nurture in makeshift nurseries on the mountainsides. Farrer's biographer, Nicola Shulman, says, 'He was considered to be a maniac by most people. He really was going to places where no westerners had been seen before.'

As a result of his travels Farrer introduced many new plants to Britain including the Himalayan Rhododendron, several varieties of bamboo and the Geranium Farreri, which was named in his honour.

Having brought his treasures back to Yorkshire, Farrer was nothing short of attentive to all of the plants in his nursery. He declared, for example, the *Primula spicata* must be 'sat up with night and day when in flower, that it may be prevailed upon, with food and flattery, to set seed'.

Farrer was much acclaimed for his plant expeditions and seemingly he got on famously with 'the natives', but his manner back home was not so highly appreciated. He dismissed many notable rock gardens of the day as 'almond-pudding schemes' and was said to be something of a snob. He also developed a reputation for being ill-mannered and ostentatious.

While always devoted to his garden, there was a time when Farrer thought he could cut the mustard as a novelist and poet. He could not. Instead, rather sensibly, he took to writing about gardening, at which he was extremely successful. His book *My Rock Garden*, first published in 1907, was continuously in print for the next forty years and his *English Rock Garden* is still the rock gardener's bible. In all Farrer wrote more than twenty books and hundreds of articles and thousands of letters.

1907 was also the year that Farrer converted to Buddhism which appealed to his 'craving for a reasonable and coherent view of the scheme of things'. To his family and friends his conversion only confirmed what an odd fellow Reginald was. (Not that they really needed much persuasion.)

Reginald Farrer's influence can be seen in many British gardens and around Ingleborough there is a most fitting memorial to the man known as the 'Father of Rock Gardening'. In a much reported incident of its day, Farrer loaded a shotgun with exotic seeds and fired them into a rock face near the hall. Nearly a hundred years on his legacy is still thriving in a wonderful array of Himalayan plants growing wild amongst the Yorkshire vegetation.

Botany and Bedouins

In the middle of the tower blocks and sophistication that is modern Kuwait, there is an old blue and white house on Arabian Gulf Street. Now a cultural centre, the house was for more than sixty years home to the formidable Dame Violet Dickson.

When she first arrived in the city in 1929 it was as Mrs Harold Dickson, wife of the new British Political Agent to Kuwait. The Dicksons' married life had begun ten years earlier when the then Captain Dickson had whisked his new bride off to Mesopotamia where her lifelong fascination with the Middle East took root. There followed time in Bahrain, Iran and Iraq before she and her husband – by now Colonel Dickson – arrived in Kuwait to be greeted by the eleven people who made up the ex-pat population.

As the newcomer in town, Mrs Dickson set about learning all there was to know about Kuwait and in time, it is said, she built up an 'unparalleled grasp of the feuds and rivalries festering among the kingdom's 600 strong royal family'.

Her interests, however, stretched well beyond court gossip and she was a frequent visitor to Bedouin encampments in the desert. Indeed, while she never learned to read or write Arabic she spoke it fluently, albeit a form of Bedouin dialect.

As a girl growing up in Lancashire the young Violet had spent much time collecting butterflies and searching the estates, where her father was the agent, for new and exciting plants. When she arrived in Kuwait she continued her search.

She scoured the desert to send plants back to Kew Gardens and in recognition of all her work the desert flower, *Horwoodia Dicksoniae*, was named in her honour – which rather surprised Mrs Dickson who did not realise she had found a totally new plant at all. As far as she was concerned the flower was not rare as it was relatively common in Kuwait. 'I wasn't even thinking of that, really, although I'd read that the ambition of all starting botanists is to find something that has never been found before.'

Her fascination with the flora of the desert led her to write *The Wild Flowers of Kuwait and Bahrain* (which she illustrated herself) and for years she kept up the search for flowers to send to Kew.

When Colonel Dickson died in 1959, his wife decided that she would stay put in the sun-dried mud house that had been her home for thirty years and continue her love affair with the Arab world. It would appear that the Arabs, in turn, took her to heart. Dame Violet, as she became in 1976, always preferred the company of men and unusually for a woman, she was frequently welcomed at all-male gatherings to discuss the news of the day. Her Bedouin friends even honoured her by calling her 'Umm Kuwai' or Mother of Kuwait.

Her lifestyle apart, no one would describe Dame Violet as a glamorous woman. She was very large, had a wardrobe of shapeless dresses, was fond of ankle socks and flat shoes and always had her hair scraped back in a bun – often topped with the obligatory cotton sunhat.

A pragmatic woman, she accepted that her chosen way of life might be considered unusual. 'Probably people think I'm rather eccentric. You don't know what other people think of you, do you? But as you see I'm quite happy here.'

Dame Violet stayed on happily in her house on Arabian Gulf Street until she was evacuated to Britain at the time of the Iraqi invasion in 1991. Sadly, she died before Kuwait was liberated. Her home, however, although ransacked and looted during the war, has been refurbished and has become the Dickson House Cultural Centre.

Candles and Lilies

Known for being a controversial and eccentric figure, one of the past treasurers of the illustrious Royal Horticultural Society, George Fergusson Wilson, will long be remembered as the man who began what are now the Society's showcase gardens at Wisely.

Mr Wilson was an industrial chemist who had helped formulate a process for making candles out of 'malodorous fats'. The invention was the basis of the Price's Patent

Candle Company and the success of the company meant that George Wilson need never fear for lack of money.

At his home in Weybridge he turned his attention, energies and enthusiasm to gardening and following his sister's example built his own orchard house. Whether to inspire himself or the plants is not known but Wilson pinned up on the beams of the structure numerous Spanish proverbs and set to work often choosing to prune by candlelight.

He then became obsessed with lilies and bought for a song a large number of Japanese bulbs that had been retrieved from a wreck and were consequently 'sea-damaged'. Back in his orchard house Wilson set to, planting out his new treasures in old wine casks, and the results were as pleasing as they were surprising. Far from having been ruined by seawater the bulbs flowered profusely and included several new varieties that had never before been seen in England. Within a short space of time, George Wilson earned a reputation for being 'the most successful cultivator and exhibitor of lilies in the country'.

When Wilson decided to leave Weybridge and buy a property known as Oakwood, near Wisley in Surrey he was thought to have taken leave of his senses. The soil was poor, the climate erratic – the site was very windy – and the estate included ancient woodland growing on deep acid soil. Wilson, however, considered Oakwood not only a challenge but an ideal place to create 'a garden as has not been made before'.

He took to his new task with vigour and planted more than two thousand species of plants, including, of course, numerous varieties of lily. Plants were brought in from all over the world on the basis that if they could grow at Oakwood they could grow anywhere. The more difficult a plant to grow the more Wilson was determined to have it.

The popularity and fame of the garden spread and to distinguish it from another well-known garden near Newcastle, also called Oakwood, Wilson's domain came to be known as Wisley.

Wilson accepted that there was a lot of interest in his work but towards the end of his life he got rather annoyed by the interruptions. To that end, he posted a notice at the entrance which read: 'Mr G. F. Wilson requests that visitors who have cards of admission will come between three and half past four. Before this time work is interfered with, after it, the "show-er-round" is often tired'.

Wilson's death in 1902 proved to be a fortuitous event for the RHS which had been looking for years to replace its Chiswick site. (Increasing air pollution was proving to be a serious problem for the prized plants.) In 1903 the philanthropist, Sir Thomas Hanbury, who had made his fortune from Chinese silk and tea, stepped in. He bought Wisley and presented it to the Society as a new garden.

Out of this World

A Grave Conceit

The Vauxhall Spring Gardens in London had already been open to the public in London for more than sixty years when Jonathan Tyers of Surrey took on the twelve acres for the sum of two hundred and fifty pounds a year in 1728. During his tenure Vauxhall enjoyed new popularity and attracted thousands of visitors keen to experience the entertainments provided by Tyers and his cohort of friends that included such luminaries as the painter William Hogarth.

Tyers was always looking for new amusements and one of the most popular events ever to be staged in the gardens was the rehearsal for Handel's 'Music for the Royal Fireworks'. In spite of the fact that the run through was devoid of any form of pyrotechnics more than 12,000 people are said to have attended to hear the hundred-strong orchestra.

The following year Tyers brought even more attention to his beloved Vauxhall Gardens when he bought and demolished several houses opposite Lambeth church to provide a carriage entrance. On the first night the new access was opened the carriages queued up for more than a mile so that their owners could take their turn at enjoying the novelty of not arriving on foot.

A rotund and jovial figure, Tyers relished the reputation he earned at Vauxhall (which he eventually bought outright) as 'the master builder of delight' and enjoyed dreaming up new ways to ensure that the Gardens remained a favourite feature of the London social scene. He devised fountains and temples, colonnades and avenues, supper rooms and orchestra stands. All of which makes his choice for his private garden even more extraordinary.

In 1754 Tyers bought the country estate of Denbies near Dorking in Surrey and set about transforming what was a modest farmhouse into a fine Georgian mansion. When it came to landscaping the garden, however, Tyers shunned the conventions of the day and took a completely different direction. Instead of creating sweeping vistas and serpentine lakes, Tyers decided to create 'The Valley of the Shadow of Death' around his new home. The gateposts to the garden were the first clue as to what lay beyond. They were shaped like coffins and each topped with a human skull – a real human skull. (There was one male skull which it was claimed was that of a notorious highwayman, and the female skull on the opposite post was said to be that of a famous courtesan.)

There were various other gruesome statues including one of a Christian and another of a non-believer, both sculpted undergoing grisly deaths. The temple at the centre of the garden was adorned with gloomy and depressing inscriptions and the clock that resounded throughout Tyers' garden struck every minute to remind those within earshot of their inevitable fate.

When Tyers died in 1767 the estate was sold and not surprisingly the new owner was not enamoured of his predecessor's taste. The garden was demolished.

Today Denbies is the largest vineyard in the United Kingdom.

Cosmic Concerns

If you think of an eccentric as someone who is out-of-step with convention (be it decades behind or light years ahead) and who indulges his or her whimsical side, then the American architect, architectural historian, designer, author, academic and landscaper, Charles Jencks, must fit the bill. He created with his late wife, Maggie Kershaw – an authority on Chinese gardens – 'The Garden of Cosmic Speculation' on her family's estate in Dumfriesshire. There can be few gardens to equal it.

Jencks describes the garden as 'a landscape of waves, twists, and folds, a landscape pattern designed to relate us to nature through new metaphors presented to the senses'. In reality that translates into a landscape that has been moulded to represent various aspects of the universe and modern scientific theory. There is the black hole terrace, a DNA and six senses garden, the fractal terrace, the snail mound, the universe cascade and countless other visual metaphors. The symmetry break terrace, for example, is where 'the history of the universe is conceived as four breaks in symmetry' and forms part of a 'giant soliton wave that wraps around the house'. Trying to fathom how Jencks wants us 'to understand cosmic processes and how we are connected to universe and nature' is not always obvious to the uninitiated and one suspects that 'The Garden of Cosmic Speculation' is not for the timid.

Moneybags and Mysticism

The lovely town on Sintra nestled into the mountains twenty-five kilometres west of Lisbon in Portugal boasts more than its fair share of extravagant buildings and gardens. The summer home of Portuguese royalty for centuries, Sintra has also attracted several fabulously wealthy men with eccentric tastes. Not least is Antonio Augusto Carvalho Monteiro, who, having amassed a dazzling fortune through his family's exploits in coffee and precious stones in Brazil, chose Sintra to build his dream home. To help him in the task he employed the Italian theatre set designer, Luigi Manini, renowned for his work at La Scala in Milan.

The two men drew inspiration from all over Europe, including the nearby Pena Palace, a magnificent and sumptuous Victorian folly of a castle built as a love nest for Maria II by her doting husband. But while the Pena Palace is more like a child's dream idea of a castle, Quinta da Regaleira has a far more mystical quality. There are still turrets and crenallations galore but 'Money Bags Monteiro', as he was known, set out with a broader vision to combine Portuguese mythology with Gothic, Rococo, Manueline and Renaissance styles and to 'glorify everything sacred'.

Certainly he did nothing to curb Manini's dramatic tendencies and the garden at Quinta da Regaleira is full of fountains, caves, terraces, grottos, gargoyles and lakes – all said to be deeply symbolic of some aspect of sanctity, masonry or the occult.

One of the most extraordinary elements of the garden is the Initiation Well, sunk sixty feet into a rock promontory on the estate. The well was designed to reflect the mysterious initiation rites that Knights Templar had to undergo and a vast colonnaded spiral staircase leads down nine levels to an underground cave. At the centre of the cave, on the floor, is carved a cross of the Knights Templar – the powerful medieval order of military monks known as the 'Militia of Christ'.

As money was never an issue, plants and trees were brought in from all over the world and mixed in with the native vegetation. In parts the gardens are formal, elsewhere wild and surprising, yet everywhere is a feeling of mystery and mysticism.

The magnificent Quinta da Regaleira was finished in 1910 and 'Money Bags' Monteiro had only ten years to enjoy it. He died in 1920 and gradually his creation fell into disrepair. Towards the end of the twentieth century the estate was named a UNESCO World Heritage Site and work began to save the mystical Quinta da Regaleira for posterity. One suspects that Antonio Augusto Carvalho Monteiro would approve.

The Trouble with Hermits

The Romantic Movement, which took hold in the late eighteenth and early nineteenth century in Britain, had its roots in literature, but in landscape terms it signified a move away

from Classicism and formality towards a more 'naturalistic'
approach. Painshill, near Cobham in Surrey, is considered to be
one of the most important gardens of the period.

It was the creation of a young nobleman, Charles Hamilton,
who having done his 'Grand Tour' returned to England set
on creating a garden that would stir the emotions of all
who saw it. He began by leasing a strip of land on the edge
of a moor near the River Mole and with borrowed money
(the family coffers were insufficient for his plans) he set
about making a theatrical landscape.

One of Hamilton's first steps was to create a thirty-acre
serpentine lake fed from water from the Mole, and then he
began on the building. There was a wood, plaster and
papier-mâché Temple of Bacchus, the carefully constructed
ruins of an 'abbey', a Gothic temple, a Turkish tent and a
Chinese bridge. Hamilton also spent large sums of money
on the planting. Many new and rare shrubs were introduced
and it was said that Painshill had the most varied collection
of conifers in the world.

There was only thing missing. It had become rather
fashionable to have a hermitage and, of course, Hamilton
had built a rather splendid one complete with an upstairs
sleeping chamber. The only problem was that the hermitage
lacked a hermit. An advertisement was placed and perhaps
not surprisingly there was not a lot of interest.

Life as a hermit was not easy. The common terms of
employment were that the appointed hermit would stay in

the hermitage for seven years, 'wearing a camel-hair robe, studying the Bible, thinking great thoughts, and being civil to visitors'. It was against the rules for the hermit to leave the garden or cut his hair, beard or nails during his tenure. In return, at the end of seven years, the hermit would receive the princely sum of seven hundred pounds. Unfortunately, Hamilton's man was a bit of a beer drinker and as alcohol was strictly forbidden it proved to be something of a stumbling block. Within the month Hamilton found his 'hermit' down at the local inn and his employment was terminated therewith. In spite of various efforts to find a replacement the post remained vacant.

Under the circumstances it was probably just as well as Hamilton was not really in a position to pay £100 let alone £700 to anyone. He tried a variety of schemes to make Painshill a paying concern – there was a vineyard that produced a more than passable sparkling wine – but none brought in the money needed to keep Painshill viable. In 1773 the friends who had financed Hamilton called in their loans and Hamilton had to sell up. He repaid his creditors and moved to Bath where he died thirteen years later at the age of eighty-two. In spite of his restricted means and limited space in his new home Hamilton was an avid gardener to the end.

After Hamilton had left Painshill the property passed through a number of hands and in 1948 was sold off in lots. What remained of the garden was left to its own devices until in the early 1980s the Painshill Park Trust was formed to save Hamilton's vision for the nation. The Trust bought

158 acres and started on an ambitious restoration project. There has been extensive work done and the project has been cited as being 'one of the great success stories of garden conservation'.

Surrealism and Boa Constrictors

Edward Frank Willis James, who died in 1984, is known for being a generous patron of the arts and the 'last English eccentric on the grand scale'. His biographer, John Lowe, in his vivid and intriguing portrayal, *Edward James, A Surrealist Life* says, 'You did not *know* Edward. He was a *happening* which you lived through, sometimes like a dream, often like a nightmare.'

Certainly, James's life was never ordained to be ordinary. It was long rumoured that he was the illegitimate son of his god-father, Edward VII, but James insisted that rumour was wrong and that it was his mother who was the king's illegitimate daughter and he, therefore, the grandson. The story, however, does not bear close examination. What is true is that Willie James – Edward's mother's Anglo-American husband and accepted as Edward's caring father – died when Edward was only four. In Willie's will provision was made for his wife and daughters but Edward was to inherit everything else on his twenty-fifth birthday. He was destined to be a very wealthy young man.

It was this endless supply of money that eventually allowed Edward to play out his passions by building an amazing garden in Mexico. He first visited the country in 1944 and fell in love with it and a young Mexican man, Plutarco Gastelum. The relationship eventually led to the creation of the extraordinary Garden Las Pozas at Xilitla, in central Mexico, a project that was to fill much of Edward's life. (Apparently Edward James once confessed that he had always had too much money and too many choices and thought that, had life been different, he would have become a gardener.)

He was originally drawn to the area under the promise that there were fabulous orchids around the small town. Although the orchids were not in bloom when Edward fist visited Xilitla, what he did find convinced him that it was the perfect spot for a lavish semi-tropical garden. Initially he and Plutarco lived in a collection of huts but the latter found the mountainside inhospitable and instead built himself a house in the village. The house (in which Plutarco still lives) would do Disney proud but is nothing compared to the garden that rises up the mountain beyond the village.

It has been estimated that James spent in excess of $10,000,000 on the site. Thousands of orchids from Hawaii and Guatamala were brought in to supplement the local varieties and the lush jungle vegetation, and hundreds of workmen and gardeners were employed. When it came to building, Edward's surrealist fantasies were indulged to the extreme, aided by the fact that few of the structures were ever completed before he moved on to the next. Consequently there are staircases that lead nowhere, doors that do not open, towering columns that support nothing, and windows that frame only the jungle. Many of the structures would do Salvador Dali proud, which is appropriate as Edward James was a long-time patron and friend of the surrealist painter.

To inhabit his paradise Edward James decided to buy exotic animals and birds and there is any number of stories about his exploits. One in particular relates to a boa constrictor that Edward bought in the back streets of Mexico City. The advice was to let the snake get used to the sound of his voice as, once accustomed to the sound of its new master, the reptile could be controlled. Back at the hotel Edward fed his snake on live mice and then persuaded it to coil itself around the bedpost while he sat up all night reading *Gulliver's Travels* aloud.

The arrival of so many animals back at Xilitla meant that cages were needed, and again architectural fantasy took over. According to John Lowe, 'The peons carried Edward up and down the steep steps in a homemade sedan chair, Edward in an old Etonian blazer with a macaw on each shoulder.' (It must be said the workmen were paid good wages to do so and never seemed to have taken offence at their employer's eccentricities.)

Although he spent part of every year in Mexico, James never really lived there and it was left to Plutarco (who in the course of his long friendship with Edward had married and sired four children) to carry on the dream that is Las Pozas.

The Paths of Righteousness

There can be few gardens that have been designed to tell the story of John Bunyan's *The Pilgrim's Progress* and to encourage the visitor to heed the philosophy of an eighteenth-century Swedish scientist, philosopher and theologian – but one that does exist is near Macclesfield.

The garden of Hough Hole House was originally the work of James Mellor, a wealthy cotton-mill owner, who devoted nearly sixty years to creating his allegorical garden. Mellor had been brought up a Methodist but later in life switched allegiance to the teachings of Emanuel Swedenborg, a man who believed 'that he should faithfully write, publish, and disseminate the heavenly truths that were revealed to him by the Lord'. For the pious Mellor, Swedenborg's philosophies had a resonance that he could not ignore. Religion dominated Mellor's life. He even arranged it that he could wake each morning to sacred music. There was a lever beside his bed which, when pulled, set off a mechanical organ that was, in turn, powered by a waterwheel secreted in a cave below the house.

He was equally ingenious in recreating the journey that Bunyan's hero, Christian, made through life. As you would expect that journey began at the Wicket Gate, which at Hough Hole was literally that at the side of the house. From there led the 'straight and narrow path', which made its way to the stable block that Mellor renamed the House of the Interpreter (the modern owners use the building as a garage).

All of the important sites mentioned in Bunyan's work were represented in the garden. Mellor's home became The House Beautiful, the next door farmhouse was Doubting Castle (where Christian encountered Giant Despair), there was Hill Difficulty, the Valley of Humiliation, the Valley of the Shadow of Death and all the others, including the Celestial City, which in Mellor's garden was a small building that doubled as an observatory and chapel.

Mellor paid close attention to the planting and he only ever planted a tree if it was mentioned in the Bible. He was also diligent in ensuring that those who toured his garden experienced a taste of hell. To that effect, he built a small stone hut with a large fireplace and small iron grating on the back wall. When Mellor was expecting visitors the fire would be stoked up with a generous addition of sulphur and an Aeolian harp would be hung outside the grating. Thus, when anyone opened the door they would be met with intense heat, a foul smell and 'piercing cries' – the screech of the harp's strings created by the rush of air.

Mellor loved showing visitors around the garden and would accompany them on the 'paths of life' preaching as he went and reciting excerpts from the Bible or passages from Swedenborg's writings.

The good man's work continued up until 1891, when he died aged ninety-six. The glories of Hough Hole House were ignored until the property was bought by a Mr and Mrs Gordon Humphreys in 1978. Their tireless work and devotion to restoring Mellor's garden means that once again the visitor (on special days only) can trace Christian's journey and follow in the footsteps of an extraordinary Victorian believer.

Waterworks and Solitude

In the early part of the seventeenth century an ingenious water garden was developed at Enstone in Oxfordshire. It was the work of a most unusual man, Thomas Bushell.

The use of water to create surprises and jokes had long been common in Europe – the most famous at the time being the Fuggers' Garden at Augsburg in Germany – but Bushell's garden was a novelty in England.

One of the delights was a rainbow room, which was a chamber from the roof of which tumbled varied streams of water. If you stood in the right position, the fall of sunlight through the showers would create scores of rainbows to surround you. There was also any number of curious fountains, one of which involved a jet of water spouting from a large rock at the bottom of a hill. The jet could rise and fall to about nine feet and on top was a silver ball which rose and fell with the water, much to the amusement of all who watched.

Between the fruit trees and beds of flowers was the highlight of the garden – a water hedge that rose to about six feet. The challenge lay in passing through the hedge and by all accounts it provided much entertainment. According to a Lieutenant Hammond who visited Enstone in 1635, '...sometimes fair ladies cannot make the crossing, flashing and dashing their smooth, soft and tender thighs and knees by a sudden enclosing of them in it'. Such delights for Hammond (and one assumes various other gentlemen) caused him to write that Enstone was a 'mad gimcrack' but 'a most pleasant, sweet and delightsome place'.

It was not only the wandering Hammond who was impressed. King Charles I and his royal entourage visited Enstone and were so taken with it that Charles decided it should be named in honour of his queen, Henrietta. (In gratitude the queen later sent Bushell an Egyptian mummy as a thank-you present.)

On the day that the royal visitors came to Enstone they were greeted with much singing and poetry and by Bushell dressed as a hermit. The choice of disguise was particularly appropriate since, just before moving to Enstone and creating his wondrous water world, Bushell had indeed been a hermit on a small island off the Isle of Man, known as the Calf of Man.

Bushell, who had once been an employee and protégé of the disgraced ex-Chancellor, Francis Bacon, had several years earlier decided to follow the teachings of his former master and '... resolved to make a perfect experiment upon myself, for the obtaining of a long and healthy life, most necessary for such a repentance as my former debauchedness required'. To that end he built, on the highest point of the Calf on the edge of a steep cliff, a small one-roomed hut where he lived on a meagre diet of 'herbs, oil, mustard, and honey'. He stayed on Calf, much to the confusion of the Manxmen, for three years until, as he put it, 'Divine Providence called me to a more active life'.

Bushell's idea of a more active life was building his waterworks and curiosities at Enstone. Then once they were complete, Bushell moved on to develop a new method of soap-making before becoming the King's Master of Mines. When Charles faced pressure from the Parliamentarians, Bushell proved to be a loyal Royalist. He formed his miners into a regiment, paid for all their clothing personally and put up £40,000 to support the King's cause.

What happened to Bushell in later years is obscure, although it is thought that when he died at the age of eighty he was penniless. Nonetheless his service to the house of Stuart was duly recognised and Thomas Bushell was buried in the cloisters of Westminster Abbey.

Herbaceous Borders and Unrequited Love

Walmer Castle in Kent is the official residence of the Lords Warden of the Cinque Ports and has been for the best part of three centuries. Originally built during the reign of Henry VIII to defend the realm against the feared invasion from France and Spain after Henry's break from Rome, the castle is now more of a stately home than a fort.

During the time that William Pitt the Younger was Lord
Warden he was joined at Walmer Castle by his ill-fated
young niece, Hester Stanhope, and it was she who did
much to create the gardens one can see at Walmer today.

The daughter of the eccentric Lord Charles Stanhope,
Hester grew up in an aristocratic but unusual household.
Her father was a confirmed Republican and after the
French Revolution insisted that he should be known
thereafter as 'Citizen Stanhope'. When he sold off the
family's carriages for being 'symbols of privilege', the young
Hester took to walking everywhere on stilts, telling her
father it was 'the only way she could keep her petticoats out
of the mud'.

While Hester may have been fortunate to inherit a strong
will, a vivacious nature and a fierce pride from her father,
her early life was blighted by the death of her mother and
then the introduction of a stepmother who was not
interested in Hester or her siblings. When Lord Stanhope
died leaving his family impoverished because he had given
away his fortune to various good causes, Hester's uncle,
William Pitt the Younger, was delighted to have her join his
household.

At the time she moved to Walmer Castle Hester was
suffering from a broken heart. Not only had she lost her
father but she had fallen madly in love with Lord Granville
Leveson Gower whose affections were otherwise engaged.
To ease her pain, Hester took up landscaping and devoted
her pent-up passion to creating beauty from the 'utilitarian

oblong' that was the Walmer garden of the day. Her uncle assisted her with her plans and soon colourful borders sprang up against dark yew hedges, and a water garden and woodland walk were added. And, while the garden was conventional, the young woman who created it was to live an exceptional life.

Within all too short a time, William Pitt died leaving Hester alone once more, although he kindly asked Parliament before he died to provide her with an annual pension, which was duly forthcoming.

There followed an engagement which was soon called off and then Hester captured the heart of England's commander-in-chief in Spain and Portugal, Sir John Moore. Before they could be married, Sir John was killed in battle, 'her name on his dying lips'. To compound her loss, one of Hester's brothers died in the same campaign. For Hester enough was enough and she decided to follow what she believed to be her fate. She set sail to Constantinople with a small entourage.

Hester's plan was to ingratiate her way into the court of the French Ambassador and convince him to allow her to travel to France. Once in Paris she would inveigle her way into Napoleon's court. That done she would uncover the workings of the Emperor's mind and then hotfoot it back to England with all the information that would help the British forces overthrow the tyrant. Unfortunately the British Ambassador got wind of Hester's plans and there was nothing for her to do but leave Turkey.

Dean is a study of stately gardens, Hicks's private garden was described as an 'unofficial memorial' to the difficult and erratic James. Yet subsequent projects designed by Hicks suggest that the cottage garden was as much a testament to his own skill and creativity as it was homage to his friend.

Hicks enjoys letting trees and shrubs grow untamed through the sculptural elements of a garden – and at West Dean there were plenty to choose from, all of which had enjoyed a different existence in an earlier life. Two former mannequins were cut off and placed at the foot of the spiral mound at the centre of the lawn. Beautifully and intricately painted, one became the 'Sky Lady', the other 'The Green Man'.

At the top of the mound sat a stack of beehives. Two painted shoe lasts 'tiptoed' across the grass and metal springs were liberally spread among flower beds, while trees were hung with the glass droplets from an old chandelier. A plastic lobster sat upon a painted chair, and mirrors were plunged into the pool. And so it went on. But Hicks is a gardener and his West Dean garden was not just a place of fun and fantasy. He trained initially as an aboriculturalist and when he came to West Dean a tulip tree came too.

Over the years, on the occasions when James allowed Ivan Hicks a rest from their adventures or when there was a momentary lapse in his demands, the tulip tree was joined by a Serbian spruce, a magnolia and various other specimens including a giant redwood.

Photographs of the Hicks garden in the late 1980s show a place that for all its oddities is bursting with drama, light and colour and the skill of the plantsman is plain for all to see.

After he left West Dean in 1990, Hicks moved to Stansted Park where he created another surreal fantasy which he called 'The Garden in Mind', and has since woven his magic into Groombridge Place near Tunbridge Wells and Escot Park in Devon, to name but two.

Ivan Hicks says he thinks a garden should be 'a place of fantasy, mystery, excitement, humour and even shock' and certainly he has done much to bring joy and humour out into the open.